CiTY

ATLAS

Illustrations by
GIULIA LOMBARDO

Text by
FEDERICA MAGRIN

WSkids
WHITE STAR KIDS

CONTENTS

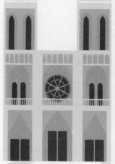

MUMBAI
PAGE 62

HONG KONG
PAGE 64

BEIJING
PAGE 68

SHANGHAI
PAGE 66

SEOUL
PAGE 72

DUBAI PAGE 60

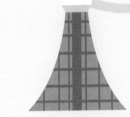
SYDNEY
PAGE 78

WASHINGTON D.C.
PAGE 86

CAPE TOWN
PAGE 58

TOKYO PAGE 74

NEW YORK
PAGE 82

MEXICO CITY
PAGE 88

CAIRO PAGE 54

BUENOS AIRES
PAGE 94

TORONTO
PAGE 80

JERUSALEM PAGE 52

RIO DE JANEIRO
PAGE 90

Hello there! Eric and Iris here. We are brother and sister and we travel a lot. We have visited the world's most amazing cities with our family and what you are about to read is a recap of our trips.

You will not find dates and notions in this book, but instead lots of interesting information and our impressions of the most famous monuments, museums and squares, and also strange and curious facts about the different places we visited. What's more, we will give you suggestions about some fun activities not to be missed. Would you like some examples?

Did you know that you can board a real aircraft carrier in New York or solve a case like a real private detective at London's Sherlock Holmes Museum?

Also, for the more important cities, we have gathered intriguing information on the customs and traditions of the various countries and some more unknown legends. We can't wait to tell you all about them!

But, before you start, you should get some equipment ready. You can't travel without a suitcase (or a backpack even better), comfortable clothes for both warm and rainy weather, a camera to capture everything, binoculars for surprise sightings, a notebook to write everything down in, and a great itch to explore.

Are you ready for some adventure? Turn the page and let's go!

The world is waiting for you!

HOW TO READ THIS BOOK...

Whether you want to discover the cities in the order we visited them, or whether you prefer to jump from one continent to another, following your love of adventure, in every map you will find some instructions to help you discover interesting places and useful information with just one glance. Look beside the name of the city and you will see its position on the map of the country where it is located. And there is the country's flag!

After reading our description of the city, you will always find these three symbols that accompany the information:

alongside the globe there is the name of the country you are in.

what language do the city's inhabitants speak? Find out here!

how many people live here? If there are less than 1,000,000 – as many as that may seem – we can define it a "small to medium-sized" city.

A "big" city has from 1,000,000 to 10,000,000 inhabitants.

If there are over 10,000,000 inhabitants it can definitely be defined a "megalopolis"!

Now you have all the information you need to start exploring. You can begin by looking on the map for numbers that refer to interesting places that we have visited and experienced. These are the first step towards getting to know the city and to set out on your unforgettable and unique adventure!

LISBON

The best way to get around the city is by tram. On our first ride, on the legendary number 28, we went up to the Alfama neighborhood and visited São Jorge Castle. We also enjoyed the extraordinary panorama on view from the Miradouro de Santa Luzia. Going back down to the lower part of the city, we took another tram to get to the monumental Jerónimos Monastery and, from there, we went by foot to the Monument of the Discoveries and the Tower of Belém. After gobbling down some amazing pastries, *pasteis de belem*, we went back to the city center to try the famous Santa Justa Lift. Even though it was a short ride, it was worth the while to see a unique view of Lisbon. Before ending the day with some excellent food accompanied by a show of the traditional Portuguese music, *fado*, we went to the MAAT - Museum of Art, Architecture and Technology to have some fun with science.

 Portugal   Portuguese   Medium-sized city

1. Go up the Santa Justa Lift for a unique view of the city.
2. Take the Gloria funicular up to Bairro Alto.
3. Wander around the ruins of the abandoned church of the Carmo Convent.
4. See if you can recognize the explorers in the Monument of the Discoveries.
5. Ride through the streets of the Alfama neighborhood on the legendary tram 28.
6. Take a photo of the city from above at the Miradouro de Santa Luzia.
7. Stroll along the battlements of São Jorge Castle.
8. Go see a traditional *fado* show.
9. Be spellbound at the MAAT - Museum of Art, Architecture and Technology.
10. Go on the hunt for mummies and other curious artefacts at the Calouste Gulbenkian Museum.
11. Brave the cold water of the ocean and dive in at Cascais beach.

MADRID

Madrid is a *muy caliente* (very warm) city. Not so much and not only for its summery climate, which is really boiling, but for the liveliness and warmth that visitors are welcomed with. Strolling through its streets, with its open-air bars and street artists to entertain the tourists, we immediately felt like we were in a party atmosphere. As well as walking the length and breadth of the city through its parks and squares, including the magnificent Plaza Mayor, we went to see the works of art filling the rooms of the Prado Museum and admired the treasures of the Royal Palace and the city's main churches: the Basilica of San Lorenzo and the Almudena Cathedral. In the evening, after a tasty *bocadillo de jamon* (ham sandwich), we went to see a captivating flamenco show. *Olé!*

 Spain   Spanish   Big city

1. Lose yourself in the magic of the music and colors at a flamenco show.
2. Visit the Bullfighting Museum to see the elaborate clothes worn by bullfighters.
3. Eat something in the company of the many cats at the Gatoteca.
4. Watch a soccer match from the stands of the Santiago Bernabeu.
5. Urge on the street artists during their exhibitions in Plaza Mayor.
6. Admire the movements of the soldiers at the changing of the guard at the Royal Palace.
7. Row a boat across the Estanque Grande in Parque Retiro.
8. Put your foot on Km 0 in Puerta del Sol.
9. Take a photograph of the statue of Miguel de Cervantes in Plaza de España.
10. Stroll along the Walk of Fame in Calle Martín de los Heros.
11. Let yourself be swept away to a fairytale world while you eat a cake at El Jardin Secreto.

BARCELONA

We had so many things to see in Barcelona that we didn't waste a second. We went straight away to explore the Ramblas – the city's streets – and then wandered around looking for Gaudi's buildings, each more magical than the next. Then we went to visit the Sagrada Familia and walked among the wonders of Park Güell to fully appreciate the architect's creativity. After a lunch of *tapas*, really tasty snacks, we went to the old neighborhood of the Barri Gotìc and then went to admire the Palau Reial. Just before sunset, after shopping at the Boqueria market, we took the cable car up to Castell de Montjuïc to enjoy a view over the entire city.

Spain   Spanish, Catalan   Big city

1. Have a picnic among the mosaic-covered terraces of Park Güell.
2. Lift the Champion's League trophy at the Camp Nou.
3. Wander among the funny chimneys on the roof of Palau Güell.
4. Climb aboard the ship of Don Juan de Austria at the Museu Marítim.
5. "Swim" under the long tunnel at the Aquarium in Port Vell.
6. Ready to set sail on-board a Golodrina? The sea awaits you!
7. Go into the courtyard of Casa Milá and look up. Isn't it amazing?
8. Stop to admire the skills of the street artists on the Ramblas.
9. Ready to climb the tree of life at the CosmoCaixa museum?
10. You needed a tasty break. Go to the Museum of Chocolate!
11. Climb the towers to get a view from on-high at the Sagrada Família.
12. Take a photograph of the Christopher Columbus monument.
13. Watch the dancing waters at the Magic Fountain in Montjuïc.
14. Visit the Automaton Museum at Tibidabo Amusement Park.

11

A CATHEDRAL UNDER CONTINUAL CONSTRUCTION

At first glance, the Sagrada Família looks like one of those sandcastles you used to make when you were small by letting wet sand slide through your hands. In actual fact, its structure is rather complex and is based on the ambitious design of an eccentric architect, Antoni Gaudí, who didn't succeed in finishing it before he died in 1926. The construction continued according to his instructions, but it still hasn't been completed today. Many people believe that it will remain unfinished forever.

THE PARK OF WONDERS

Apart from the Sagrada Família, Antoni Gaudí left numerous other works to Barcelona: Casa Milà, Casa Batlló, Palau Güell, etc. All characterized by the imagination of this architectural genius. Perhaps the artist's most surprising creation is Park Güell, a garden where vegetation and art unite in a perfect whole. Strolling around admiring the columns that imitate trees to then come out into real woods is something magical. The centerpiece of the park is the terrace bordered by a bench covered in mosaics from where you can admire the unusual buildings located at the entrance, along with the city itself.

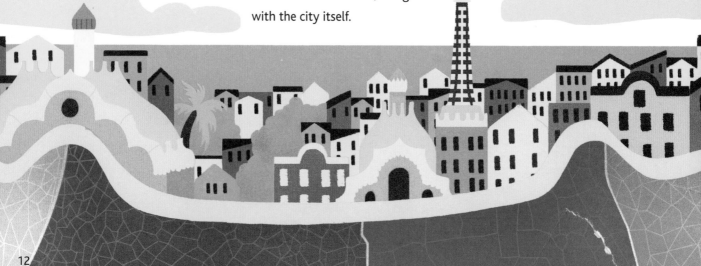

Human castles: this is how the *Castells* are defined. They are made of teams of people with others standing on their shoulders, creating towering pyramids. This is a very popular tradition in Catalonia, the Spanish region where Barcelona is located, where various teams compete against each other to form ever higher human towers. The amazing thing is that, once the *Castell* has been built, it does not stay still. Instead it moves to the rhythm of traditional music. Don't try it with your friends though – it could be dangerous!

SKY-HIGH HUMAN TOWERS

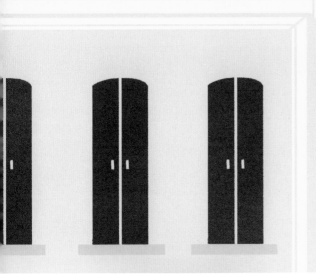

THE GREAT CHILDLIKE ARTIST

Spanish artists are a bit like their country: full of colors and life, creative and original. Perhaps the most famous is Pablo Picasso, who is considered the fathers of the Cubist movement. If you look at one of his paintings from this period, you will see they are a bit like children's pictures. So, he was criticized heavily for this, but his response silenced everyone. Picasso said, "It took me a lifetime to paint like a child", meaning going back to that spontaneous way of creating that you lose as an adult.

PARIS

The Eiffel Tower: this was the starting point of our tour of the wonders of Paris. From the top of this imposing construction, you get a unique view of the city of love. Our cruise down the River Seine by *bateau-mouche* (fly boat) was also romantic. The river flows along between famous monuments, such as Notre-Dame, the Louvre, and Muséè d'Orsay. After a break to eat crêpes for lunch, we went to explore the enormous *boulevards,* the broad streets of Paris, and then stopped off at Montmartre, the artists' district, to admire the Sacré-Cœur Basilica and see the exterior of the famous Moulin Rouge. When evening approached, it suddenly became clear why Paris is also known as *Ville Lumière,* the city of lights. It was like a huge illuminated carnival, brimming with color and life.

🌍 France   🗣 French   👫👫 Megalopolis

1. Fly over the city in a Zeppelin and see Paris from above.
2. Create lightning at the Cité des Sciences et de l'Industrie in La Villette.
3. Do you want to be an illusionist? Discover some tricks at the Museum of Magic.
4. Explore the banks of the Seine from on-board a *bateau-mouche*.
5. Are you brave? Prove it by going to the top of the Eiffel Tower and looking down!
6. Visit the grave of the singer Jim Morrison at the Père-Lachaise cemetery.
7. Feeling tired? Take a break to eat a croissant at the Jardins du Trocadéro.
8. Try to guess who all the statues represent at Parc Monceau.
9. Roam through the rooms of the Louvre looking for the *Mona Lisa*.
10. Lose yourself among the monstrous stone figures on the towers of Notre-Dame.
11. Watch a show at France's oldest Puppet Theatre.

ACADEMIE DE

THE SECRET INHABITANT OF NOTRE-DAME

If you climb up the 422 steps leading to the top of the towers of Notre-Dame, you can walk among the gargoyles, monstrous stone figures that act as spouts to convey rainwater from the roof. And if you use your imagination, you can also see the hunchback Quasimodo, who was hopelessly in love with the young gypsy girl Esmeralda, ring the bells as he did in Victor Hugo's novel and the Disney cartoon.

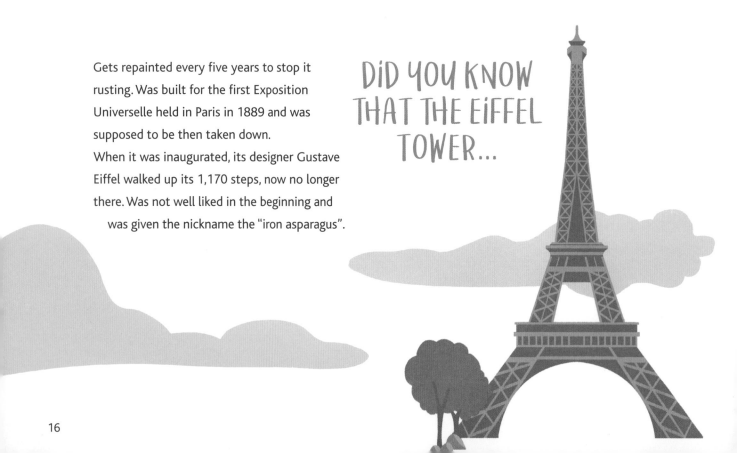

Gets repainted every five years to stop it rusting. Was built for the first Exposition Universelle held in Paris in 1889 and was supposed to be then taken down. When it was inaugurated, its designer Gustave Eiffel walked up its 1,170 steps, now no longer there. Was not well liked in the beginning and was given the nickname the "iron asparagus".

DID YOU KNOW THAT THE EIFFEL TOWER...

NOT JUST A MUSEUM

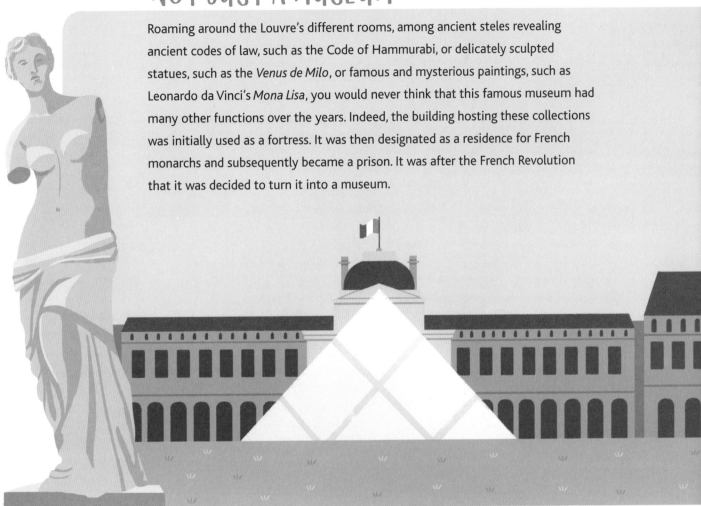

Roaming around the Louvre's different rooms, among ancient steles revealing ancient codes of law, such as the Code of Hammurabi, or delicately sculpted statues, such as the *Venus de Milo*, or famous and mysterious paintings, such as Leonardo da Vinci's *Mona Lisa*, you would never think that this famous museum had many other functions over the years. Indeed, the building hosting these collections was initially used as a fortress. It was then designated as a residence for French monarchs and subsequently became a prison. It was after the French Revolution that it was decided to turn it into a museum.

WITH THE EYES OF AN ARTIST

Explore the streets of Montmartre, still today full of artists concentrating on painting, and try to imagine what this extravagant neighborhood must have been like in the Paris of the late 19th century, with night clubs, shows, dancers, etc. Do you need a hand? Look at the paintings of Henry de Toulouse-Lautrec who dedicated most of his works to this world of artists and misfits. It was he who painted the advertising boards of some of Montmartre's entertainment spots, such as Le Chat Noir and the Moulin Rouge.

MADAME TUSSAUDS

18

LONDON

When we arrived in London, the first thing we did was go up the London Eye and... Wow! From there we could see the Palace of Westminster, where the Parliament has its seat, Big Ben, the Thames, and the Tower of London along with the adjacent bridge. The view of the city was even more spectacular higher up, ranging as far as the furthest neighborhoods. Back down again, we caught the Underground to rush to Buckingham Palace – the Queen's residence – for the changing of the guard! Then we headed off on a double-decker bus to go shopping at Portobello market. Tired and famished, we bought some fish and chips and ate them on a bench in Hyde Park. Finally, we dove into the confusion of Trafalgar Square and then went to the theater: a Shakespeare play was just what we needed!

 United Kingdom   English   Megalopolis

1. Listen to the ringing of Big Ben's bells in front of the Palace of Westminster.
2. Solve a case at the Sherlock Holmes Museum.
3. See if you can fit through the narrowest street: Emerald Court.
4. Cheese! Take a photo with Iron Man at Madame Tussauds.
5. Wait for a ship to pass and then cross Tower Bridge.
6. Admire London from the upper floor of a double-decker bus.
7. Look down! What an amazing view from atop the London Eye!

8. Have afternoon tea at Mad Hatters.
9. Look up to see the Diplodocus at the History Museum.
10. Splash! Dive into the Thames on a Duck Tour.
11. Wander around the ancient walls of the Tower of London.
12. Give the mummies a fright at the British Museum!
13. Think of a nickname for The Shard and 30 St Mary Ax skyscrapers.
14. Witness the changing of the guard at Buckingham Palace.
15. Wander through Hyde Park looking for the statue of Peter Pan.

(7)

(11)

(9)

(8)

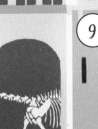

(10)

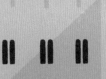

THE TOWER OF LONDON

Walking along the battlements, gardens, and rooms of the Tower of London is like losing yourself in British history. This is where many of the nation's most important events have taken place. Great monarchs lived there, such as Elisabeth the First, and famous people were locked up there. As well as being a royal residence and prison, the Tower had important functions: arsenal, treasury, and state mint. Today it is a place to get lost in while imagining how it must have been like to live in this city in the past.

THE RAVENS

Numerous ravens live at the Tower of London, and it is believed that they protect the monarchy!

ROYAL OSTENTATION

Take a deep breath before you enter the Crown Jewels museum, because later you will be left breathless. Everywhere you turn, you will see scepters, crowns, rings, and other precious objects. The crown of Queen Elizabeth Bowes-Lyon features the famous Koh-i-Noor which, for a long time, was the largest diamond in the world.

THE BEEFEATERS

In the past, the Yeomen Warders, or guardians of the Tower, defended the crown jewels. They are also known as Beefeaters because they could have all the meat they wanted. They were also in charge of looking after the crows, who, it is said, protect the monarchy.

TRAVELING WITH HARRY POTTER

Ready to leave for Hogwarts? You just need to go to platform 9 and ¾ at King's Cross Railway Station. There you will find the Express train for the world's most famous school of wizardry waiting for you. But watch out, it is an imaginary platform that "muggles" cannot see!

A SPOONFUL OF SUGAR...

Look up towards the sky. Is that Mary Poppins up there? It was in London where the nanny of the famous Walt Disney musical came flying down. Not many people know that in the original book, written by Pamela Lyndon Travers, Mary Poppins was anything but sweet and nice.

OH ROMEO, ROMEO...

What better theatre than London's Globe to watch Romeo and Juliet's eternal declaration of love? Even though this play is set in Verona, Shakespeare is strongly linked to London and its ambience. The Globe Theater, a reconstruction of an Elizabethan theater, is the perfect place to relive his dramas.

AMSTERDAM

Exploring the streets of Amsterdam city center, we immediately realized that everyone travels around by bicycle in this city. So, we too jumped on a saddle and, being careful of the more experienced cyclists, we went looking for the most important monuments. We visited the Basilica of Saint Nicholas, the Rembrandt House, and the Carré Theatre, and looked at the Royal Palace from the outside. After resting for a while among the stalls of the flower market - pedaling is tiring! - we got back on our bikes and dedicated the rest of the day to visiting two unmissable museums: the one dedicated to Van Gogh and the museum where Anne Frank's house stood.

Netherlands   Dutch   Medium-sized city

1. Wander through the old city streets on a bike.
2. Go around the many canals of Amsterdam by boat.
3. Visit the attic of the Anne Frank House and Museum.
4. Relax with an open-air concert at the Vondelpark theater.
5. Ready for strong colors? Check out the florescent art of Electric Ladyland.
6. Try to make enormous bubbles at the NEMO Science Museum.
7. What a beautiful smell! Immerse yourself in the floating flower market.
8. What do you think about living in a floating house?
   Find out how at the Woonboot Museum.
9. Admire the beauty of the city from the Westerkerk bell-tower.
10. Diamonds! Watch them being cut at Coster Diamonds.
11. See the *Sunflowers* up close at the Van Gogh Museum.
12. Cross the Magere Brug, a wooden drawbridge.

BERLIN

We decided to start our visit to Berlin at its most famous symbol, the Brandenburg Gate. We passed underneath it to admire this construction in all its majesty. From there, we went to the extremely modern Potsdamer Platz with its spectacular Sony Center. Then we moved on to the equally famous Alexanderplatz where we saw the World Clock (Urania Wetltzeituhr) and the Fountain of the Peoples' Friendship. Tired but satisfied, we ate a wurstel sandwich in the shade of the trees in the Tiergarten and visited the zoo. In the afternoon, we went to see the remains of the wall that once divided the city and then ended our extraordinary day by going to the top of the Television Tower and admiring the city at sunset.

Germany   German   Big city

1. Try your driving skills with the mini cars at the Legoland Discovery Centre.
2. Relax by watching the gentle giant pandas at Berlin Zoo.
3. Find out all about the *Achaeopteryx* fossil at the Natural History Museum.
4. Do you like fairy tales? Go see the fountain dedicated to them at Volkspark Friedrichshain.
5. Touch the remains of the Wall that used to divide the city of Berlin.
6. If you like computers, the Technikmuseum is for you!
7. Play at being a puppet master at the Puppet Theatre Museum.
8. Test your science skills at MACHmit.
9. Sail on the waters of Wannsee on-board a whale-shaped boat.

When you think of visiting the Berlin Wall, which used to divide the city in two parts, you would expect to feel sadness and a sense of anxiety, but instead the youth of Berlin have found a way to transform this symbol of hate and separation into lively, colorful murals. The graffiti that cover the wall are not just works of art, but also a sign of hope for a nation that has managed to be reborn and recreate itself. The nearby park, Mauerpark, is an oasis of relaxation where you can enjoy the performances of acrobats and jugglers.

A WALL OF ART

FAIRY-TALE WATER FEATURES

Puss in Boots, Little Red Riding Hood, Hansel and Gretel... If you are looking for a fairy tale written by the Brothers Grimm you need to go to Berlin's Volkspark Friedrichshain. In this green oasis, you will find the Märchenbrunnen, the fountain of fairy tales, decorated with the statues of some of the more famous fairy-tale characters. Frogs, dogs, dolphins, and other animals also peep out from among the jets of water, making the atmosphere of this surprising work of art even more magical.

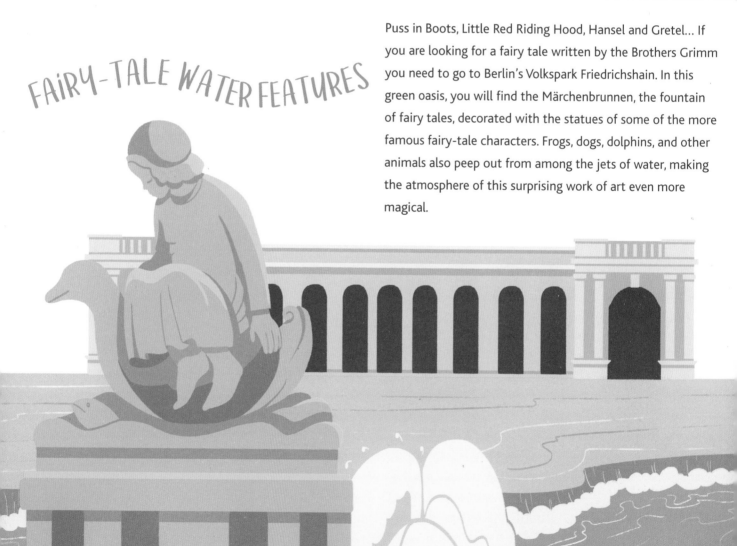

FRIENDSHIP AND THE WORLD IN A SQUARE

Go to the center of Alexanderplatz and look around you: you will see gigantic buildings that are not that aesthetically pleasing. Not much else is visible among the confusion of passers-by. And yet, this square more than any other represents a period of history that the city, now looking to the future, cannot forget: the time when the Wall divided the East from the West. This is the case for the buildings and the Television Tower, but also for the important signs of opening up to the world such as the World Clock, which shows the time in various countries, and the Fountain of the Peoples' Friendship.

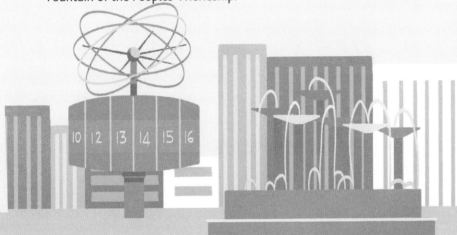

THE EINSTEIN TOWER

Albert Einstein is one of the most famous scientists and is also greatly beloved of people who have nothing to do with science. Perhaps this is because we think of him in the photo where he sticks his tongue out and because it is often said that he was not exactly a model student. Basically, he feels like one of us! However, we must not forget that it is to him we owe the theory of relativity, which is vital to understanding how the universe works. One way to honor his memory is by visiting the Einsteinturm, an astrophysics observatory that was dedicated to him at the start of the 20th century.

EXPERIMENTARIUM CITY

COPENHAGEN

As soon as we started exploring its streets, Copenhagen immediately seemed like a fairy-tale city; the city center is lively and colorful, and at the port you can take a picture with the Little Mermaid, the protagonist of the Danish writer Hans Christian Andersen's most famous story. No less magical is the panorama you can enjoy by taking a boat tour among the canals, especially when you see the extraordinary reflection of the lively houses of the old port Nyhavn in the water. After we got off the boat, we went walking down Stroget to get distracted by the street artists at the side of the avenue. After that, we went to Rosenborg Castle and Amalienborg Palace to dive into the life of the royal court. Tired and hungry, we then sat down to enjoy a Rode Polser, the Danish version of a hot-dog. With new energy, we turned to more recreational activities, playing with science at the Experimentarium and stroking the baby sharks at the Aquarium. Then we soared up above the enchanted trees at Tivoli Gardens onboard a hot-air balloon. What an experience!

 Denmark   Danish   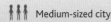 Medium-sized city

1. Ride a beast among the dragon rollercoasters at Tivoli Gardens.
2. Take a fairytale selfie with the Little Mermaid in the background.
3. Visit the Aquarium to touch a harmless baby shark.
4. Make huge soap bubbles at the Bublearium on the second floor of the Experimentarium.
5. Take a boat ride among the colorful houses of Nyhavn facing out onto the canal.
6. Watch the changing of the guard in front of the Amalienborg Royal Palace.
7. Let yourself be enchanted by the puppets along Stroget, the main avenue of the historical city center.
8. Find out if it is going to rain: look at the statues of the barometer on the corner of the Town Hall.
9. Imagine being a Viking at the children's section of the National Museum of Denmark.

WARSAW

Warsaw surprised us. We had read that it had been completely rebuilt after the Second World War and so we were expecting a super-modern city. But it's not! There certainly are new buildings and skyscrapers, but those who looked after the reconstruction made sure that the city went back to being the same as in the past, with houses of fading colors and sloping roofs. Crossing the city to get to its more important buildings, such as the Castle and Wilanów Palace, was like diving into a timeless world. After spending some time in the Old Town Market Place and admiring the performances of the street artists, we went on a lovely cruise on the Vistula river and then admired the exterior of the Gothic Cathedral and entered into the Church of the Holy Cross where the composer Chopin's heart is conserved. Finally, we couldn't miss visiting what's left of the Jewish Ghetto, walking along the Memorial Route to honor an important part of the history of this city.

 Poland   Polish   Big city

1. Take a photo beside the Mermaid in the middle of the Old Town Market Place.
2. Roam among the fountains and statues in the gardens of the Wilanów Palace.
3. Walk down the 16 blocks of granite of the Memorial Route.
4. Listen to a concert below the Chopin monument at the Lazienki Park.
5. Go up to the terrace of the Palace of Culture and Science for a spectacular view.
6. Enjoy a science show at the Copernicus Science Centre.
7. Go on a unique trip on the Kolejki Waskotorowe steam train.
8. Go down into the Castle's underground which is full of archeological remains.
9. Sail along the Vistula on a boat.

31

PRAGUE

Lots of people had told us and we realized for ourselves shortly after arriving: there is something magical about Prague. Perhaps the atmosphere is due to the numerous legends about the city, but actually, walking down Golden Lane, strolling through the Old Jewish Cemetery or crossing Charles Bridge, we had the feeling that there, behind a house, tombstone or statue, we too would have found the mysterious Golem that is said to be still hidden in the city. In the end, we did not have any supernatural encounters, but we came across extraordinary monuments, such as the majestic St. Vitus Cathedral or the Tower of the Old Town Hall with its much-cherished clock. What was really incredible was seeing the city divided in two by the Vltava river from up in Malá Strana. It is a fairytale landscape!

Czech Republic   Czech   Big city

1. Watch the movements of the little statues in the Astronomical Clock.
2. Take a ride on the city's historical tram: the number 91.
3. Stroll down Golden Lane: the street of the alchemists.
4. Visit the tombs of the Kings of Bohemia in the crypt of St. Vitus Cathedral.
5. Look for the legendary Golem in the cemetery of the Jewish Ghetto.
6. Check out the strange form of the Dancing House.
7. Admire how glass is molded at the Moser factory.
8. Take a photograph of the upside-down statue of King Wenceslas at Lucerna Café.
9. Try to measure the castle's enormous Vladislav Hall.
10. Look for the statue of the knight Bruncvik with his lion on Charles Bridge.

BUDAPEST

As this city is crossed by the "blue Danube", we couldn't resist starting with a cruise down the river to admire all of its splendor. From the boat, we had a unique view of both the majesty of the Parliament Building and the beauty of the Chain Bridge. Back on land, we took the funicular up to the upper part of the city and immersed ourselves in Buda Castle's rooms, full of historical memories. Then, to honor the Hungarian city's past, we walked through Memento Park with its collection of 42 statues from the Communist era. After a break at a pastry shop to try the *Dobos* chocolate cake, we got on a tram to Margaret Island, where we rented bikes to explore the length and breadth of the island and, in the evening, we watched the music fountain that lights up with different colors.

Hungary   Hungarian   Big city

1. Ride the Siklò funicular to Buda Castle.
2. Cross over the Danube by the Chain Bridge.
3. Take a photograph of the statue of the Archangel Gabriel in Heroes' Square.
4. Have fun at the Palatinus Bath on Margaret Island.
5. Taste a delicious *Dobos* cake at a pastry shop in Vaci Utca,
   the most famous pedestrian street in Budapest.
6. Enter into the fairytale atmosphere of the rooms of Parliament.
7. Set sail on a cruise along the blue Danube.
8. Admire the old vehicles at the Hungarian Technical and Transportation Museum.
9. Discover the subjects of all the statues in Memento Park.

VENICE

Water is everywhere in Venice. In fact, we could say that the canals are considered roads there. You can also stroll along the paved *calli* and *campielli*, but we decided to visit the city by vaporetto (ferry) and we even treated ourselves to a tour in a gondola. We passed under Rialto Bridge and saw palaces such as Ca' Foscari mirrored in the water beneath us. Obviously, we couldn't miss out on the famous Saint Mark's Square with its Basilica and Campanile, but the best part was losing ourselves among the little stores, buying Murano glass animals and trying on Carnival masks. This is the magic of Venice: diving into the centuries-old traditions of a city floating on a lagoon.

Italy   Italian   Medium-sized city

1. Climb on-board a gondola and cross the Grand Canal.
2. Watch a glass object being made in Murano.
3. Visit the Doge's Treasures at Palazzo Ducale.
4. Pass through the extremely narrow Calletta Varisco: it is 20 inches!
5. Admire the Pala d'Oro on the altar in Saint Mark's.
6. Buy a souvenir from the little stores on Rialto Bridge.
7. Stroll through the most ancient Jewish Ghetto.
8. Relive the splendor of the 18th century at the Ca' Rezzonico Museum.
9. Look for the 13 lions in Saint Mark's Square.
10. Look out the tiny openings in the Bridge of Sighs.
11. Visit the ancient prisons at Palazzo Ducale.
12. Try your hand at rowing in the water in front of the Arsenal.
13. Discover Venice through binoculars from atop Saint Mark's Campanile.
14. Watch how Carnival masks are made at a workshop.
15. See the Moors striking the hours at the Clock Tower.

ROME

Strolling around Rome, we immediately realized that every last corner of the city tells something of the past. After walking through the streets of the Forum, where the Ancient Romans would meet to debate, and gaping at the size of the Colosseum, where gladiators would fight fierce animals, we headed to the Circus Maximus, the ancient horse track, and the Thermal Baths. There we thought that it must have been relaxing to immerse yourself in the baths as they did in the past. After a break at one of Trastevere's restaurants, we did a tour of Renaissance Rome, gazing up at the ceiling of the Sistine Chapel and then visiting the amazing Saint Peter's Basilica.

Italy   Italian   Big city

1. Lights, camera, action! Relive famous movie scenes by visiting Cinecittà's magnificent sets
2. Throw a coin into the Trevi Fountain and you will come back to Rome!
3. Peep through the keyhole on the Aventine Hill... Oh look, it's the dome of Saint Peter's!
4. Get your photo taken with a gladiator in front of the Colosseum.
5. Do you tell the truth? Find out by putting your hand inside the Mouth of Truth.
6. Stand on the stones of the ancient Roman road, the Appian Way.
7. Cover your ears when the canon is fired at the Janiculum!
8. Go into the mini projection room in the Cinema dei Piccoli at Villa Borghese.
9. It's so hot! What you need is a *grattachecca*, Rome's version of a snow cone!

CINECITTÀ

FiGHTiNG TO THE DEATH

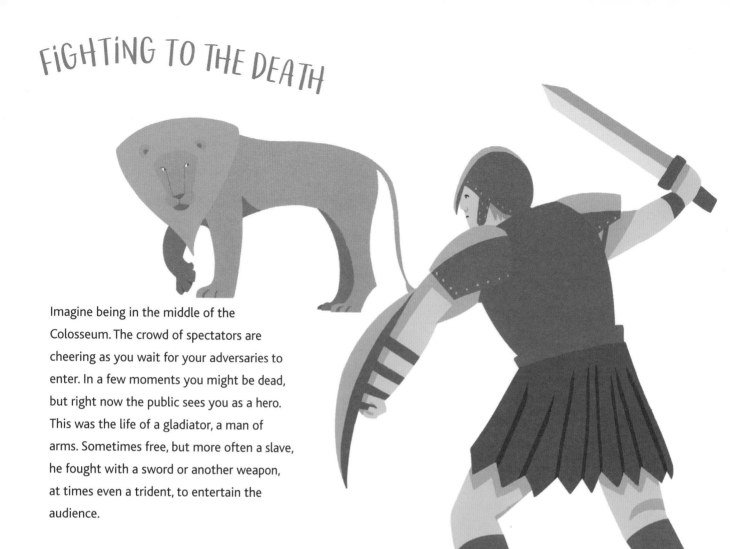

Imagine being in the middle of the Colosseum. The crowd of spectators are cheering as you wait for your adversaries to enter. In a few moments you might be dead, but right now the public sees you as a hero. This was the life of a gladiator, a man of arms. Sometimes free, but more often a slave, he fought with a sword or another weapon, at times even a trident, to entertain the audience.

YOU'D BETTER TELL THE TRUTH!

If you were told that if you stuck your hand into a mouth and told a lie it would be bitten off, would you do it? This is the legend of the Mouth of Truth, a marble mask of a Roman deity, probably once used as a drain cover. It now hangs on the wall of the atrium of the Santa Maria in Cosmedin Church. The legend goes that the mask can tell if someone is lying and eats their hand.

Approximately 2,000 feet long and roughly 390 feet wide... When the Ancient Romans built something, they thought big! The Circus Maximus, a vast oval-shaped circuit still visible today, was used to hold chariot races in ancient times. Twelve quadrigas (chariots drawn by four horses) would race in front of approximately 250,000 spectators. There were also stores, taverns, and baths to provide the public with some refreshment. Like a modern-day stadium!

A GIGANTIC CHARIOT RACETRACK

A WOLF FOR A MOTHER

Legend has it that Rome was founded with the incredible story of two twins: Romulus and Remus. Abandoned in a basket and left to the mercy of the waters of the Tiber, they were miraculously saved from the river by a she-wolf who looked after and nourished them. The bronze statue of a she-wolf at the Capitoline Museums represents this legend.

MUSEUM

ATHENS

The Parthenon: this is where we started our tour of Athens. It is the center of the Acropolis, the upper part of the city. The most famous temple of ancient Greece enchanted us with its majesty and beauty. From here we could look around at the roofs of the city below us and even glimpse the sea on the horizon. We then went back down to the lower part to visit the Agora – an ancient square – where we tried to imagine what it would have been like to live there in the past. When we got tired of playing pretend, we went to find a restaurant to try some *moussaka*, made from eggplants and cheese. Then well rested, we went to Syntagma Square to see the changing of the guard and then on to Monastiraki Square to buy some souvenirs at the market stalls. In the evening, we watched the sun set from the Port of Piraeus.

Greece   Greek   Big city

1. Wander among the columns of the Parthenon on the Acropolis.
2. Stroll among the ancient monuments of the Agora.
3. Go to a show at the Odeon of Herodes Atticus.
4. Eat traditional seafood dishes at Mikrolimano port.
5. Go to the stadium of Panathinaikos, where the first Olympics were held.
6. Walk among the stalls at the market in Monastiraki Square.
7. Pet the cats that roam the streets of Anafiotika.
8. Eat hanging in the air on the Dinner in the Sky.
9. Discover the hidden wonders at the National Gardens.
10. Test your skills at the Hellenic Children's Museum.

THE SONG OF HEROES

Sing, goddess, the anger of Peleus' son Achilleus. These are the opening words of *The Iliad*, the Greek poem by Homer that tells about the destruction of the city of Troy. In the middle, there are arguments among the gods, fights to the death, betrayals, and intrigues. In the poem, the goddess Athena, founder of Athens, is the protector of Achilles, the greatest Greek hero.

FROM THE TOP OF OLYMPUS

When you are touring around Athens, try to avoid pestering any deities because the Greek gods can be both good and cruel at the same time. You should know that people used to believe that Zeus, Athena, Hera, Apollo, and all the other many gods up on Mount Olympus did not always stay there quietly, but instead often came down to Earth to poke their noses into human affairs. After all, it gets a bit boring sitting on top of a mountain after a while.

The Parthenon was built according to classical architectural standards which made it an unrivalled work of art. This can also be seen from its impressive numbers: it was made with 13,400 blocks of marble; it was decorated with a frieze showing events in low relief that was about 520 feet long; it had a statue of the goddess Athena in gold and ivory that was 39 feet tall; it had eight columns on the short sides and 17 on the long sides that were roughly 33 feet high.

THE SIZE OF A PERFECT TEMPLE

ANCIENT AND MODERN GAMES

In the modern Olympics, held for the first time in Athens in 1896, there are sports that had not yet been invented in Ancient Greece, such as basketball and fencing, but some of the sports are the same as those that were played in the Olympic city between 776 BC and 393 AD, such as running and javelin throw. You might not know this, but athletes used to compete naked in classical times and women were not allowed to watch from the stands. The modern version is better, don't you think?

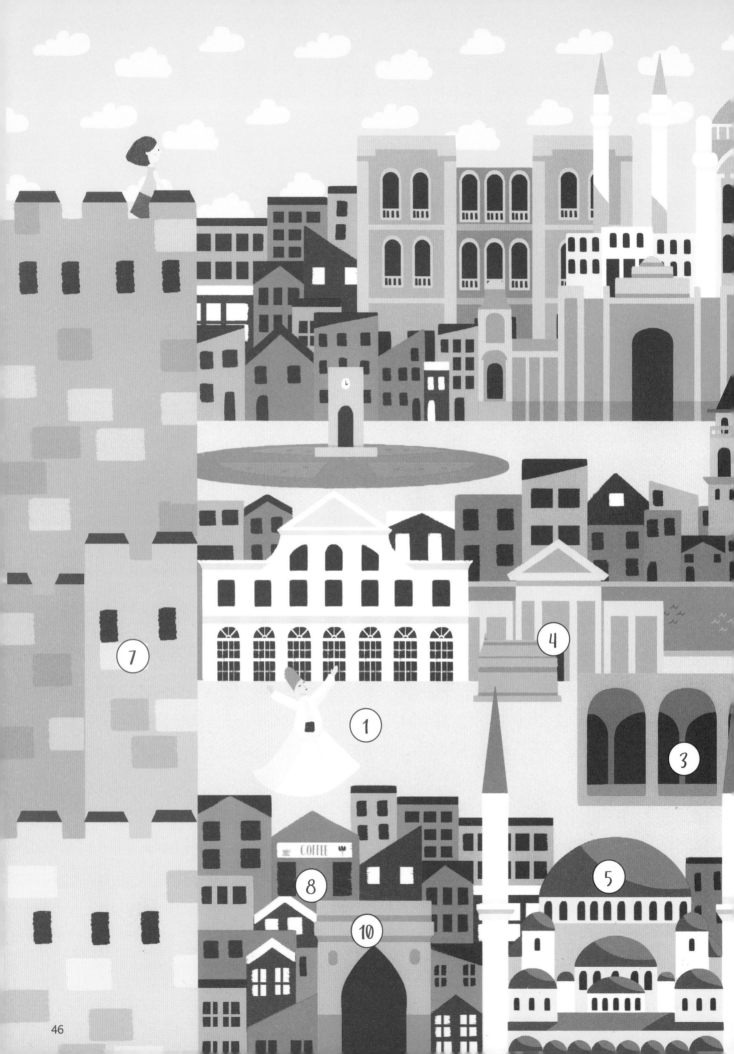

ISTANBUL

The Bosphorus – the strait between the Black Sea and the Sea of Marmara – is what has made Istanbul what it is: a city divided between Europe and Asia. So, we started by crossing this stretch of sea by boat in order to dive into the mix of cultures that makes the city so unique. After visiting Hagia Sophia, we walked along the Walls of Constantinople, a route which gives you great views of Istanbul from above, and admired the decorations of the Blue Mosque. The most amazing part was wandering amongst the stalls of the Grand Bazaar, where we were blown away by the shouts of the vendors, the aromas of the spices, and the colors of the rugs. In the evening, we went to see a show of whirling dervishes. In the end, our heads were spinning too!

 Turkey   Turkish   Megalopolis

1. Watch the extraordinary spinning of the whirling dervishes.
2. Sail along the waters of the Bosphorus on-board a boat.
3. Explore the semi-darkness inside the ancient Roman cistern.
4. See Alexander the Great's sarcophagus at the Archaeological Museum.
5. Admire the majolica tiling inside the Blue Mosque.
6. Try to recognize the people depicted in the mosaics of Hagia Sophia.
7. Have a relaxing stroll along the Walls of Constantinople.
8. Taste Turkish tea in a tulip-shaped glass.
9. Discover some traditional Turkish games at the Toy Museum.
10. Immerse yourself in the scents and colors of the spice bazaar.

MOSCOW

Moscow immediately came across as a majestic city to us. We saw this walking through Red Square, surrounded by the high walls of the Kremlin Palace, and with a unique glimpse of Saint Basil's Cathedral. This building particularly grabbed our attention: the colorful onion-shaped domes reminded us of ice-cream cones. Also, the lavish subway with its decorated stations is worthy of a nation with such an illustrious history. However, given that Moscow is not only a hub of art, but also science, after a lunch of crepes called *blini*, we ventured into the rooms of the Museum of Paleontology to look for mammoths, and then went to the Memorial Museum of Cosmonautics for a full immersion into the history of the exploration of space. For a fitting ending to our tour of the city, we went to the Bolshoi Theater to see a Russian ballet show.

Russia   Russian   Megalopolis

1. Go to see the traditional Russian circus Nikulin.
2. Look for the space dogs Belka and Strelka at the Memorial Museum of Cosmonautics.
3. Immerse yourself among the conifers full of squirrels at Losiny Ostrov National Park.
4. Take a photo of the Tsar Cannon and the Tsar Bell at the Kremlin.
5. See the changing of the guard at the Kremlin.
6. Wander through the labyrinth of chapels at Saint Basil's Cathedral.
7. Go for a bike ride through the gardens of the Exhibition of Achievements of National Economy.
8. Enter into the magical atmosphere of the Bolshoi Russian ballet.
9. Admire the colors of the matryoshkas at the Izmailovo market.
10. Look at the mammoth skeleton at the Museum of Paleontology.
11. Take a trip down the River Moskva with a trolleybus.
12. Be an astronaut with a model space ship at Gorky Park.

When you take a subway, you expect to board an underground train that will quickly transport you from one part of the city to another. The Moscow subway does this and much more. Some of the stations are not simply places to wait for a train to arrive, but instead are like art galleries. One example is Komsomolskaya with its grand yellow ceiling embellished with mosaics, not to mention Ploshchad Revolyutsii, with a collection of as many as 70 bronze statues or Elektrozavodskaya, lit up by an impressive number of circular lamps.

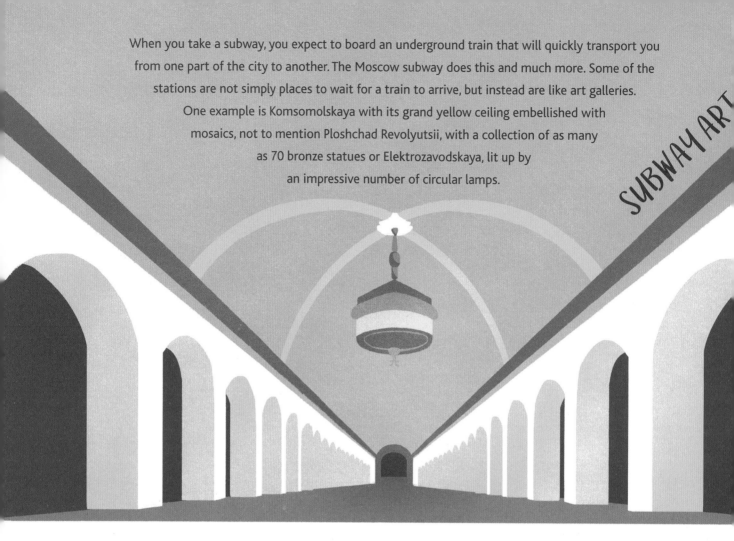

STARS INSTEAD OF EAGLES

The towers of the Kremlin palace shine with red five-pointed stars, but it was not always like that. In the past, at the time of the Tsars, there were two-headed eagles in place of the stars. After the October Revolution, these symbols of power were replaced by stars. If you look at them from below they might all seem the same, but they aren't. This is because they made them different sizes in proportion to the height of their respective towers. Clever, huh?

THE "STRANGE" SAINT OF THE CATHEDRAL

The cult of Basil the Blessed is important in Russia today just as it was at the time of the Tsar Ivan the Terrible, the period when the saint was alive. Stories are told about this strange hermit that are hard to believe. People say that he used to steal from the rich to give to the poor – a bit like Robin Hood – and that he could foresee people's deaths and read their minds. This is why the Moscow cathedral is known as Saint Basil's Cathedral, even though its real name is the Cathedral of the Intercession.

MISSIONS INTO SPACE

ANIMAL

A dog in outer space? It sounds like the plot of a new cartoon or some ad created to attract people's attention. But no, the first Russian space traveler was actually a little dog. Her name was Laika and she was launched into space on November 3, 1957 on-board the spacecraft Sputnik 2 from the Baikonur Cosmodrome. At the Memorial Museum of Cosmonautics in Moscow, you can find two other space dogs: Belka and Strelka.

JERUSALEM

Jerusalem is a timeless city. Strolling among its more famous monuments is like immersing yourself in the past and diving momentarily into the political and religious events that have made this city sacred for the Jewish, Christian, and Muslim religions. And so, our tour of Jerusalem had to start at the Temple Mount where the Jewish Temple once stood and which now hosts the Dome of the Rock. The atmosphere at this peaceful place cannot be found anywhere else on Earth. From here, we then went to visit the Al-Aqsa Mosque and the Wailing Wall. After a stroll around the Arab market, full of aromas and colors, we walked down the Via Dolorosa in order to finally end our day with a visit to the Church of the Holy Sepulchre.

Israel   Hebrew, Arabic   Medium-sized city

1. Jump on the statues of animals at the Noah's Ark in the Biblical Zoo.
2. Would you be able to make a vase or press oil? Try it at the Ein Yael Living Museum.
3. If you have a wish, write it on a piece of paper and stick it into the Wailing Wall.
4. Follow the Stations of the Cross along the Via Dolorosa.
5. Try your hand at haggling among the stalls of the Arab market.
6. See the city from atop Herod's Gate.
7. Read the prayers written in all different languages at the Mount of Olives.
8. Walk among the trees at the Garden of the Righteous Among the Nations.
9. Visit the Church of the Nativity in Bethlehem, a few kilometers from Jerusalem, the place where Jesus was born!

53

CAIRO

When we arrived in Cairo, we were met by the deafening din of horns honking in the city's crazy traffic. Confusion and liveliness also accompanied us around our visit to the Khan el-Kahlili market, where the vendors' shouted offers mixed with the prayers reaching us from the minarets every now and then. Here we tried the tasty honey sweets before going to the Egyptian Museum, where we were gobsmacked by the treasures of the pharaoh Tutankhamun. Then we went on a short trip to enter the Great Pyramid of Giza and look at the mysterious Sphinx. The sun was already setting when we got back to the city, so we were just in time for a quick (and refreshing!) felucca trip on the Nile and a breathtaking view of the city from atop the Cairo Tower.

 Egypt   Arabic   Megalopolis

1. Travel the road to the Pyramids of Giza on the back of a camel.
2. Board a felucca and let the wind take you across the Nile!
3. Brave enough to face the curse of the pharaohs? Visit the Egyptian Museum.
4. Haggle for goods at the Khan el-Khalili souk.
5. Stroll in the tranquility of the Arab gardens at Al-Azhar Park.
6. Have dinner at the top of the Cairo Tower and see the city rotating around you.
7. Pretend to be an ancient Egyptian at the Pharaonic Village.
8. In Memphis, a few kilometers from Cairo, one of the colossal statues of Ramses II is preserved. Get your photo taken beside the giant reclining statue!

A MYTHICAL NAME

Cairo in Arabic is *Al-Qahir*, or "The Victorious". Do you think it refers to a pharaoh and his conquests? Given the city's past it could well be, but it actually isn't. The Victorious refers to the planet Mars, the god of war. Legend has it that astrologists were asked to make a horoscope for the city before it was built. What the scholars saw was the birth of the planet Mars. And so, the city was called *Al-Qahir*, which Europeans then transformed to Cairo.

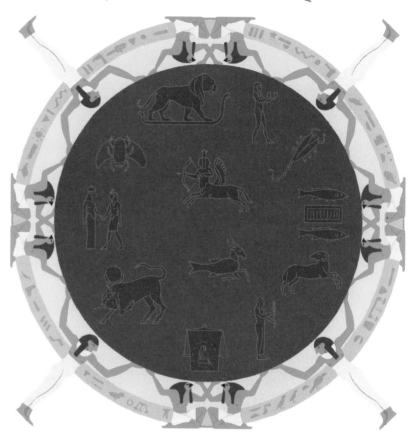

IN THE MYSTERIOUS WORLD OF THE PHARAOHS

You can easily get to Giza by car or on the back of a camel. Whatever way you chose — one is more comfortable, though less adventurous! — the surprising thing is that, though it is really close to the metropolis of Cairo, the Giza Plateau truly is another world. Leaving the modern world behind you, here you really are in the Land of the Pharaohs. The three pyramids of Khufu, Khafre, and Menkaure stand out in the desert land. These monumental burial mounds are worthy of the great ancient monarchs. Here we also find an enigmatic construction: the Sphinx, with the body of a lion and the head of a man.

AMONG THE TREASURES OF THE BOY KING

The Egyptian Museum conserves one of the most important archaeological finds of all times. Discovered thanks to the genius and tenacity of the scholar Howard Carter, the treasure of Tutankhamun includes canopic jars, caskets, sculptures, and, above all, the famous funeral mask, made with two layers of gold and embellished with colored glass and gems.
This masterpiece of goldsmith art not only represents the face of this pharaoh, who died so young, but also embodies the very image of the world in which he lived.

NOT JUST WORKS OF ART

Even if you're brave and don't believe in superstitions, the Mummy Room at the Egyptian Museum could freak you out. You can find 27 well-conserved bodies of kings and queens of Ancient Egypt there. After their death, the pharaohs and important people were reserved a complex mummification treatment, carried out by priests, which kept the bodies more or less intact. It was common belief that, in this way, the deceased could come back to life after death. So, look out for the mummy!

CAPE TOWN

While we usually start discovering a city with a tour of its monuments, we made an exception with Cape Town and focused first on its natural distinctive traits. We were curious to see its white sharks. Our encounter with these animals was incredible, and then our trip back to land gave us a unique view of the city. After enjoying a refreshment in a bar on the Victoria & Albert Waterfront, we took the cable car to the top of Table Mountain to see the panorama from above. As it was already late, we went back down to the city center to stroll through the narrow streets of Bo-Kaap and see some famous buildings, such as the Old Town House. We saved Robben Island for last: the prison island where Nelson Mandela was locked up.

 South Africa   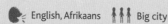 English, Afrikaans   Big city

1. Visit Robben Island, where Nelson Mandela was held prisoner.
2. Take a photo of the statues of the Nobel Peace Prize Winners in Nobel Square.
3. Take a lively stroll along the Victoria & Alfred Waterfront.
4. Go through Greenmarket Square, where slavery was abolished.
5. Look at testaments of Apartheid at the District Six Museum.
6. Walk through the windy streets of Bo-Kaap with its colorful houses.
7. Take the cable car up to the top of Table Mountain.
8. Check out the penguin colonies at Boulders Beach.
9. Pretend to be a botanist admiring the rare species at the Kirstenbosch Garden.
10. Admire the bastions of the Castle of Good Hope from above.

DUBAI

An oasis in the desert: this is how this city appeared before our eyes. You can find everything here, but just outside the city, there is only sand. Crossing its streets heavy with traffic and admiring the skyscrapers reaching up to the sky, it's strange to think that, up to recently, there was just a small settlement of nomads here. Now, on the other hand, you can enjoy all kinds of wellness and even play sports typical of other regions, such as skiing at Ski Dubai. What surprised us most was our experience going up to the top of the world's highest building: Burj Khalifa. But visiting the old city and the Gold Souk was just as exciting. It was like a return to the past in a city that seems projected towards a future fit for a science-fiction movie.

United Arab Emirates   Arabic   Big city

1. Go skiing at the amazing indoor ski facility, Ski Dubai.
2. Go to Madinat Jumerira Mall on-board a traditional boat.
3. Do you like flying? Take a seaplane for a tour of the city from the sky.
4. Try the thrill of going up the highest skyscraper, the Burj Khalifa.
5. Let yourself be spellbound by the atmosphere of the Bur Dubai spice souk.
6. Watch the water and light show at the Dubai Fountain.
7. Admire the lavishness of Dubai Mall, the world's largest shopping mall.

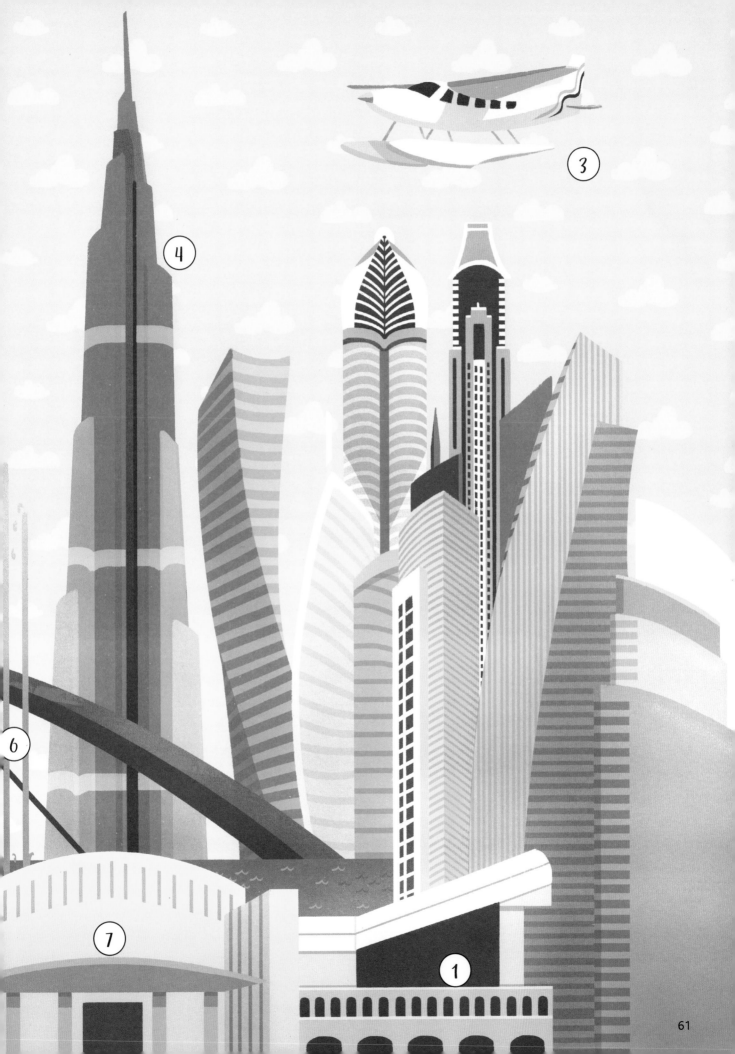

MUMBAI

We were greeted by a colors, smells, and noises galore walking through the streets of Mumbai. Everything seemed amplified and magical in this city. This feeling became even more evident at the market among the vendors selling spices and sari and at the Chhatrapati Shivaj Terminus. But we just had to venture into the Elephanta Caves to leave the confusion of the city behind us and immerse ourselves in what seemed like a world inhabited by statues of Hindu gods. After a walk around Sanjay Gandhi National Park and a tour of the open-air laundromat of Dhobi Ghat, we found some time to go into the Haji Ali Dargah mosque and the Balbunath and Siddhivinayak temples. And, obviously, our day in Mumbai had to end with a captivating Bollywood-style show.

 India   Hindi, English   Megalopolis

1. Watch a cricket match on the grassy pitches of Central Park.
2. Try to recognize the various Hindu gods in the Elephanta Caves.
3. Bring flowers as an offering to Mahalakshmi Temple.
4. Try the thrill of passing under the Gateway of India.
5. Walk along the causeway leading to the Haji Ali Dargah mosque.
6. Climb the enormous staircase of the Chhatrapati Shivaji Terminus.
7. Admire the ancient statues of the Hindu gods at the Prince of Wales Museum.
8. Wander around the stalls brimming with goods at Crawford Market.
9. Take a selfie with the gigantic Buddha at Kanheri Caves.
10. Go horse trekking along the pathways of Sanjay Gandhi National Park.

BOLLYWOOD

HONG KONG

In order to appreciate the wonders of this city, we were advised to see it from atop Victoria Peak, the mountain that overlooks the city. So, we took the tram to get to this summit, where we enjoyed an even more incredible panorama than we had expected, with the skyscrapers and the bay below our feet. Not satisfied with this experience in altitude, we went up the cable car Ngong Ping 360 with its transparent floor to see the gigantic statue of Buddha. Once we descended from this site, we took the boat out to see the Kowloon Peninsula from the water. Once again by boat, we went to the fishing village of stilt houses where we tasted amazing specialty fish dishes. In the evening, we let ourselves be spellbound by the light show at the Avenue of Stars.

Special Administrative Region of China

Chinese

Big city

1. Jump on the tram for an exciting journey to Victoria Peak.
2. Watch the "A Symphony of Lights" show from the Avenue of Stars.
3. Swim at the amazing Shek-O beach.
4. Take the Star Ferry to visit the Kowloon Peninsula.
5. Get your photo taken near the gigantic Tian Tan Buddha.
6. Visit Tai O, the village on stilts inhabited by fishermen.

SHANGHAI

At the start of our visit to Shanghai we were pretty disorientated. The city seemed to be dominated by traffic, noise, and smog. But we just needed to stop for a minute and look up high to fully grasp Shanghai's charm with its forest of skyscrapers. They are the most unexpected shapes, with buildings that look like giant bottle-openers and others that seem to defy the laws of gravity. However, Shanghai is not just a city projected towards the future, as we found out walking down the Bund, a wide road along the Huangpu river. This was like being magically catapulted to Europe with its colonial-style buildings. The city's past is even more evident in Nanshi, the Old Town, where we strolled among pagoda, temples, and markets. We even managed to witness a tea ceremony at the Huxinting Chashi, a pavilion surrounded by an artificial lake full of golden-red koi fish.

China   Chinese   Megalopolis

1. See the city from the Huangpu river on-board a boat.
2. Wander among the old engines at the Railway Museum.
3. Take photos of the Chinese tigers and golden monkeys at the zoo.
4. Visit the Volkswagen Factory to see how cars are manufactured.
5. Stroll among the mini trees at the bonsai garden in the Arboretum.
6. Go up to Cloud 9 Bar, the highest bar in the world, in the Jin Mao Tower.
7. Have tea in the rotating room of the Oriental Pearl Tower.
8. Take a photograph of the skyscraper shaped like a bottle-opener: the World Financial Center.
9. Discover the fierce-looking deities at the Jade Buddha Temple.
10. Wind around Zhujiajiao's canals on traditional boats.

BEIJING

Beijing is a city poised between the past and the future. And so, we decided not to neglect either of the city's souls. Firstly, we honored tradition by exploring the "city within the city": the imperial palace, also known as the Forbidden City, which is imbued with an air of grandeur and peace. After visiting the Summer Palace and its gardens and admiring the magnificence of the Temple of Heaven, we roamed around Tiananmen Square, the location of many of China's historical events. For a quick bite to eat, we opted for meat skewers (*chuan*) bought at the market, and then we dedicated the rest of the day to modern Beijing: the stadium (the Bird's Nest), the center for performing arts (the Egg), and the multifunctional skyscrapers.

China   Chinese   Megalopolis

1. Watch a surprising kung fu performance at the Red Theatre.
2. Take a rickshaw and lose yourself among the streets of the old city!
3. Experience the magic of the movie The Last Emperor by exploring the streets of Dashilar.
4. Cross over the stone bridge to Qionghua Island at Beihai Park.
5. Count the dorsal plates of the Stegosaurus at the Museum of Natural History.
6. Feel the thrill of walking through the Gate of Heavenly Purity.
7. Let yourself be enchanted by the acrobats at the Beijing Opera.
8. Watch people practicing Tai Qi in the Temple of Heaven.
9. Take a photo to capture the marble boat at the Summer Palace.
10. Listen to the rhythm sounded by the drummers at the Drum Tower.

红剧场
RED THEATRE

A DOG TO KNEEL BEFORE

What do you think Pekingese dogs look like? A lion or a monkey? It might seem like a strange question, but it's not. According to Chinese tradition, this dog was in fact born from the love of a lion and a monkey. The result was an animal deemed to be Buddha's protector and a guardian against evil spirits. This is why these dogs were allowed to stay in the gardens of the Forbidden City and were considered sacred, to the extent that people would have to kneel down in their presence. Just think, you could have been sentenced to death for stealing one!

Despite the legend, it not visible from space by the naked eye. It is also defined the world's longest cemetery due to the human remains that have been buried in its vicinity.Sticky rice flour was used to glue the bricks together. Its name in Chinese is *Wa-Li Qang-Qeng*, which means "10,000-Li Long Wall" (approximately 3,100 miles). Legend has it that the wails of a young woman mourning her husband made a section of the wall collapse.

THE GREAT WALL OF CHINA: DID YOU KNOW THAT...

Kung fu is a mixture of Chinese martial arts. It is not limited to just physical training, but also seeks mental balance. As is the case with many Oriental practices, where body and soul are considered a whole. We can see this in the animated movie *Kung Fu Panda*, where the lazy Po is guided on a journey of self-discovery by the wise Oogway who invites him to exercise and meditate. So, when you think of this sport, don't just picture Bruce Lee-style flying scissor-kicks!

A CROSS BETWEEN BODY AND SOUL

Now, as in the past, China is at the center of global trade. While nowadays the preferred way of transporting goods from the East to the West is by ship or plane, once upon a time it was on a camel's back. Imagine what it must have been like to travel all those miles on the back of an animal? To get an idea of how adventurous this kind of journey was, it might be interesting to read *The Million*, the tale Marco Polo (1254-1324) wrote about his experiences in Cathay (China).

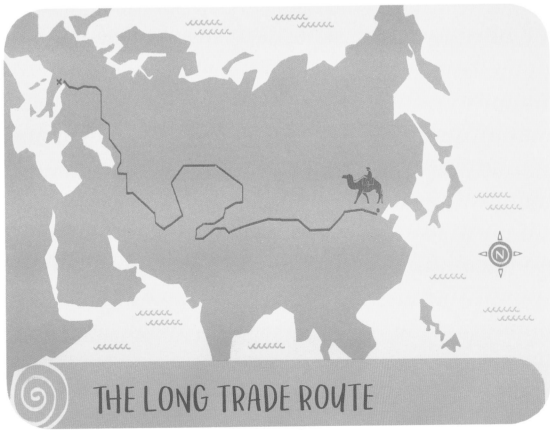

THE LONG TRADE ROUTE

SEOUL

We started our visit of Seoul on the saddle of a bicycle. Nothing better to travel the banks of the River Han which flows between palaces and skyscrapers. After this two-wheeled tour, we went to seek out modern Seoul with its futuristic buildings at Dongdaemun Design Plaza and the innovative National Museum of Modern and Contemporary Art. At Namdaemun Market we were offered fried crickets, but instead we opted for a vegetable dish, *kimchi*. It was really tasty! With our stomachs full, we went to the old part of Seoul with its Bukchon Hanok Village and Changdokgung Palace. From there we went on to visit the Jongmyo Shrine, once dedicated to worshipping the kings. Then we spent the evening Gangnam Style. Did you know that the name of that song in fact came from a trendy neighborhood in Seoul?

South Korea   Korean   Megalopolis

1. Take a bike and pedal along the River Han.
2. Attach a lock to the grid of the Tower on top of Mount Namsan.
3. Get your photo taken in front of the Gangnam Style sculpture.
4. Do you want to travel to the future? Look at the buildings at Dongdaemun Design Plaza.
5. See how a river is born at Cheonggye Plaza.
6. Pretend to be an inhabitant of ancient Seoul at Bukchon Hanok Village.
7. Get lost in the "secret" garden of Changdokgung Palace.
8. Look at the 20,000 tiles on the Wall of Hope.
9. Let yourself be enchanted by the Moonlight Rainbow Fountain.

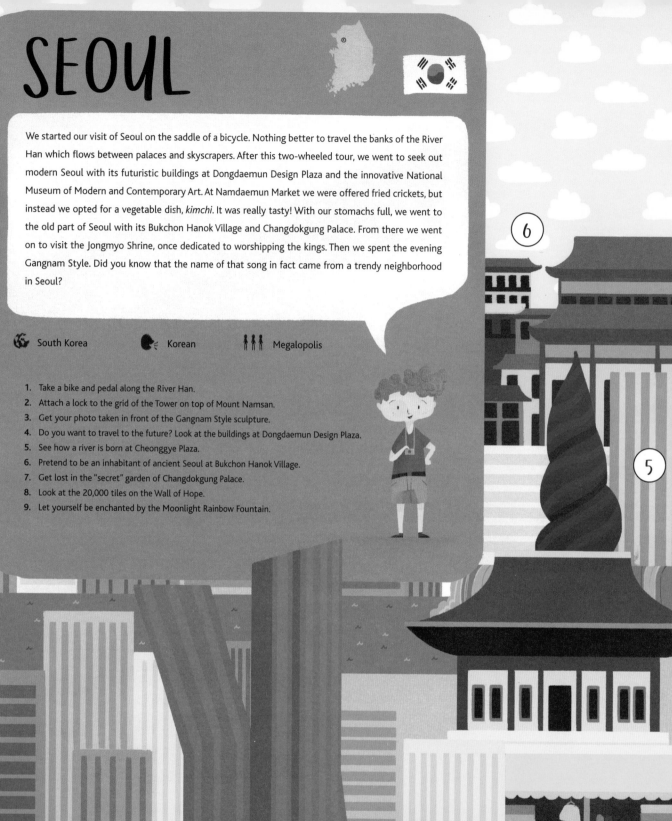

TOKYO

As soon as we set foot in Tokyo, we got the feeling of being catapulted into the future, where everything travels quickly and nothing is left to chance. Even in the neighborhoods dominated by traffic, such as Akihabara, the home of videogames, or Shinagawa, the business center, everything is incredibly clean and orderly. We first turned our attention to the modern side of the city. We went up the Tokyo Tower and saw the Tokyo Sky Tree. We browsed around the strangest bars, like those specially dedicated to karaoke, and we sneaked into one of hotels where you sleep in mini "capsules". After a lunch of excellent sushi, we then went to explore the past (the Royal Palace, the Senso-Ji Temple) and nature, with a tour among the cherry blossoms at Ueno Park. We ended our day with the colors of the Rainbow Bridge.

Japan   Japanese   Big city

1. Ride a UNI-CUB: half vehicle, half robot.
2. Lose yourself in the magical atmosphere of the Tokyo Anime Center.
3. Pass through the Thunder Gate (Kaminarimon) of the Senso-ji Temple.
4. Try the traditional Japanese baths at Asakusa Kannon Onsen.
5. Navigate the Shinobazu Pond on a swan-shaped pedal boat.
6. Admire the colors of the Rainbow Bridge by night.
7. Get your photo taken beside the statue of the faithful dog Hachiko.
8. Brave the crow at the Shibuya pedestrian crossing.
9. Show your artistic side at the Suginami Animation Museum.
10. Watch sumo wrestlers training at the Arashio-Beya gym.

A MULTI-MEDIA NEIGHBORHOOD

Are you a videogame fanatic? Do you like electronics? Are you into the world of anime and manga? If so, the Akihabara district is for you. Here you can find stores specialized in computers, videogames, and comics. A colorful world with the thrill of losing yourself in the hunt for new and rare articles. And even if you are not a big fan of the genre, these streets will surprise you with the appearance of cosplay, people dressed up as the more famous cartoon characters.

A CLOSE ENCOUNTER WITH TOTORO

There is a place in Tokyo where you can see and touch the cartoons of the Japanese master Hayao Myazaki: the Ghibli Museum. Here, along with the other characters born from the imagination of this artist, you can find Totoro. This good creature, a mix between a bear and a raccoon, guards the forest and makes friends with the two sisters Satsuki and Mei, the protagonists of the animated movie *My Neighbor Totoro*. And after seeing Totoro, you can climb aboard the "Catbus" or meet the Robot Soldier. Maybe you can also go into the Saturn Theater to watch an original short movie.

Watching a tea ceremony, *chanoyu* (hot water for tea), requires patience and concentration. In fact, it is not just about preparing this hot beverage, but rather the correct and scrupulous application of a series of gestures that refer to Zen techniques. Even the rooms are spaces that are specifically arranged to allow you to dive into a world parallel to reality, where calm rules. They are known as "emptiness rooms". It is a spiritual place where enjoying a drink is the same as freeing your mind of thoughts.

A CEREMONY TO LOSE YOURSELF IN

THE SPECTACLE OF THE CHERRY BLOSSOMS

If you take part in a *Hanami*, be ready to remain speechless. As the term (meaning "looking at the flowers") says, it involves witnessing the spring blossoming of ornamental cherry trees, called *sakura*. It is something so beautiful that it seems unreal. Even more amazing is seeing the tree branches covered in pinkish white flowers and walking on the sprinkling of petals covering the ground in the wonderful Ueno Park where there are roughly 8,000 cherry trees.

SYDNEY

In Sydney, we divided our time between culture and fun. There are lots of experiences to be had in this city, and we wanted to try almost all of them. Summoning up all our courage, we climbed up to the top of Harbour Bridge tied to safety harnesses. It was worth it – the view over the bay is incredible! We also went surfing and snorkeling, first at Manly and then at Clovelly Beach. After so much physical activity, we decided to slow it down a bit and went into the heart of the city to visit the Sydney Opera House and the district known as The Rocks. Finally, to find out more about Australian culture and nature, we went to Sydney Harbour Park, where we met a group of aborigines, and Taronga Zoo, where we saw some cuddly koalas.

Australia   English   Medium-sized city

1. Are you brave? Then climb up to the top of Harbour Bridge.
2. Put on a mask and go snorkeling at Clovelly Beach.
3. Try your hand at surfing at Manly Beach.
4. Admire the aborigine engravings at Sydney Harbour Park.
5. Check out the kangaroos, koalas, and Tasmanian devils at Taronga Zoo.
6. Go on a ghost tour in The Rocks neighborhood.
7. Visit the prison cells at the Justice and Police Museum.
8. Experience the emotion of the Scenic Cableway to the Blue Mountains.
9. Go to a fun show at the Sydney Opera House.
10. Go hunting for strange shells on Shelly Beach.
11. Go into the observatory to admire the stars of the Southern Hemisphere.
12. Lose yourself among the inventions at the Powerhouse Museum.
13. Watch the opossums jumping among the branches in Hyde Park.

TORONTO

Lots of people had told us that the Toronto skyline was spectacular. So, the first thing we did as soon as we arrived was to take the boat to the Toronto Islands. They were right: from afar, the outline of the city is amazing with its skyscrapers and the CN Tower. On the islands, we took advantage of the good weather to go on a bike ride immersed in greenery. Back in the city, we visited the Royal Ontario Museum and then Ripley's Aquarium. All that excitement made us hungry. Since Canada is famous for maple syrup, we spread it on some pancakes and devoured it all. After lunch, we strolled through the financial district and went to see the famous Casa Loma, a building that looks like a knight's castle. At sunset, we went to the top of the CN Tower to see the city light up all around us after dark.

Canada   English   Big city

1. Spend an entire day visiting the most famous waterfalls in the world: the fabulous Niagara Falls! They are not far from Toronto.
2. Get y our photo taken in "augmented reality" with the T-rex at the Royal Ontario Museum.
3. Test your courage on the Edgewalk of the CN Tower.
4. Buy some sweets made with real maple syrup at St. Lawrence Market.
5. Lose yourself in an exciting bike ride around the Toronto Islands.
6. Experience a day as a pioneer at Black Creek Pioneer Village.
7. Let yourself be enchanted by the Dangerous Lagoon at Ripley's Aquarium.

NEW YORK

As soon as we got out of the taxi, we craned our necks to see New York's famous skyscrapers. Ambling along the busy sidewalks, we crossed through this glass and steel jungle, seeking out the city's oldest buildings, such as the Flatiron, the Empire State Building, and the Chrysler Building. In the Big Apple – as this city is known – we just had to dedicate some time to shopping. After so much rushing about, we treated ourselves to a stroll in Central Park while eating a hot dog and then took the ferry out to the Statue of Liberty. We were tired, but not tired enough to miss out on a musical. So, we ended the day on Broadway to the tune of *New York, New York*!

 United States of America   English   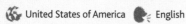 Megalopolis

1. If you're cold, warm yourself up by ice-skating at Rockefeller Center!
2. Board an aircraft carrier at the Intrepid Sea-Air-Space Museum.
3. Sail a remote-control boat at the Conservatory Water in Central Park.
4. Look, it's Balto! Take a photo with the statue of the sled dog in Central Park.
5. Challenge your mom and dad to a videogame at Nintendo World.
6. Go kayaking around the Statue of Liberty.
7. Are you afraid of heights? Summon up your courage and admire the city from the Empire State Building!
8. Get a pencil and paper and try to sketch the graffiti at the Harlem Hall of Fame.
9. Will the juggler drop the skittles? Find out at Bryant Park!
10. Pretend to be a cowboy near the bison at Bronx Zoo.

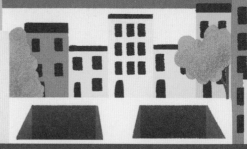

What would you do if people thought the bridge you had built could collapse? Test it, right? So, the company that built Brooklyn Bridge, in agreement with the famous circus owner P.T. Barnum, had the idea of getting 21 elephants, 7 camels, and 10 dromedaries to cross it. And so it was that, at 9:30 a.m. on May 19, 1884, spectators were treated to the unusual vision of a circus crossing the bridge.

CiRCUS CROSSING

A "BEASTLY" SKYSCRAPER

The famous Empire State Building was initially a huge failure. Even though it was a record-breaking construction (the world's highest building, the fastest to be built, and the first with a hundred floors), it remained empty for a long time. Curiously, in the end, its fame is not due to the records it broke, but rather to a large ape. In the final scenes of the 1933 movie, the monstrous King Kong climbed up the skyscraper, where he swiped at the airplanes attempting to strike him. From then on, this building has become the perfect setting for all types of films.

INSIDE LIBERTY

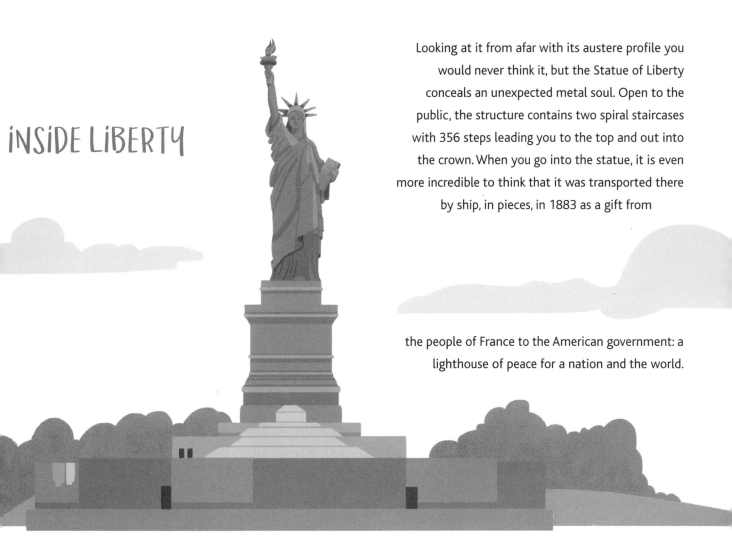

Looking at it from afar with its austere profile you would never think it, but the Statue of Liberty conceals an unexpected metal soul. Open to the public, the structure contains two spiral staircases with 356 steps leading you to the top and out into the crown. When you go into the statue, it is even more incredible to think that it was transported there by ship, in pieces, in 1883 as a gift from

the people of France to the American government: a lighthouse of peace for a nation and the world.

Have you ever heard of New York referred to as the "Big Apple"? Do you know why? It is not because it is covered in orchards or apples are eaten there a lot or because it looks like an apple. Instead, it is because that was how some punters used to call the city's race track back in the 1920s. And so, the sports journalist John J. Fitz Gerald named his column "Around the Big Apple". This nickname was made "official" during an advertising campaign of the city in 1971. Since then, the Big Apple has been synonymous with New York.

A CITY TO BE EATEN

THE BIG APPLE

1
2
3
4

WASHINGTON D.C.

This is where the history of the United States was made and where power is still administered today. We could sense this as soon as we arrived, when we took a photo of the White House – where the President lives – and strolled through the gardens in front of the huge Capitol Building – the home of the US Congress – and it was made even clearer to us when we got to know the city by touring around through the National Mall. At every corner of the city a memorial to the great men of the past awaited us. The presidents (such as Washington or Lincoln) and the most illustrious politicians (such as Martin Luther King) have had memorials dedicated to them: high obelisks and gigantic statues. Also, the Smithsonian Museum was a surprise. It was great pretending to be paleontologists, aviators, and explorers for a day.

United States of America   English   Big city

1. What about trying flight simulation at the National Air and Space Museum?
2. Could you see yourself as a spy? Try it out at the International Spy Museum.
3. Discover the world of insects at the Discovery Room in the National Museum of Natural History.
4. Get your photo taken with the statue of Abraham Lincoln at the Lincoln Memorial.
5. Read the words about rights engraved in the monument to Martin Luther King.
6. Lose yourself in books at the Reading Hall of the Library of Congress.
7. Take a horse ride around Rock Creek Park.
8. Sail down the Potomac River to see the more famous monuments.
9. Look for the Marine Corps War Memorial at the Arlington National Cemetery.
10. Look at the reflection of the large obelisk in the Reflecting Pool.
11. Chase the squirrels running around the Constitution Gardens.

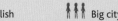

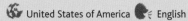

MEXICO CiTY

Mexico is color and music, and its capital city is no exception. Our tour of the city was guided by these two themes. In Plaza Garibaldi, we were greeted by mariachis who made our visit to the city center even more fun. Color was everywhere, in the Murals of Diego Rivera, the tiles of the Casa de Los Azulejos, and the rooms of the Frida Kahlo Museum. Immersed in such a party atmosphere, we also had a chance to admire the Aztec ruins at the Templo Mayor and the National Museum of Anthropology. After a siesta and a snack of nachos, we moseyed around the churches, the Cathedral, and the Basilica of Our Lady of Guadalupe, waiting for sunset to see the city from atop the Torre Latinoamericana.

 Mexico   Spanish   Megalopolis

1. Go to a *Lucha Libre* (Mexican wrestling) match.
2. Dance to the rhythm of the music of the mariachi in Plaza Garibaldi.
3. Take a paddle boat around the Lake in Chapultepec Park.
4. Take a close look at the Aztec Sun Stone at the National Museum of Anthropology.
5. Pretend to be an archeologist while wandering around the ruins of the Templo Mayor.
6. Let yourself be captivated by the Aztec dancers at El Zócalo.
7. Following local traditions, offer some cocoa beans to a Christ's statue in the Cathedral. But don't worry, sweets are also ok!
8. Relive the history of Mexico in the rooms of Chapultepec Castle.
9. Move around the Basilica to admire the Virgin of Guadalupe from every angle.

RIO DE JANEIRO

We just couldn't help it! As soon as we got to Rio de Janeiro, we took the train through the Tijuca forest to get up to Corcovado, where we admired the city at the feet of the huge statue of Christ the Redeemer. From there, we could look out over Rio's thousands of natural attractions: the Sugarloaf Mountain, Guanabara Bay, and the beaches. We headed to one of these, Copacabana beach, when we came down towards the sea. Nothing better than a game of soccer to get into the Brazilian spirit! The fact that we visited during Carnival meant we got to watch the parades of samba dancers dressed in gaudy colors from the stands of the Sambodrome. It was an experience we will never forget! *Brasil! Brasil!*

 Brazil   Portuguese   Megalopolis

1. Imitate Neymar playing soccer on Copacabana beach.
2. Enter the Tijuca forest by taking the train up to Corcovado.
3. Take the cable car to reach the top of Sugarloaf Mountain.
4. What will happen in the future? Find out by doing experiments at the Museum of Tomorrow.
5. Lose yourself in the colors of the tropical vegetation at the Botanical Gardens.
6. Get into the rhythm of the dancers at the Sambodrome during Carnival.
7. Taste some coconut milk while sunbathing on Ipanema beach.
8. Challenge your adversaries at the sandcastle contest in Copacabana.
9. Swim in the magical landscape at the red beach of Praia Vermelha.
10. Ride around the city on the legendary Bonde tram.

The Carnival in Rio de Janeiro is a serious business. Work is started on organizing it a year in advance. The city's samba schools prepare the costumes and train hard to parade inside the Sambodrome, a huge structure made of a large road called Avenida Marquês de Sapucaí, where the dancers show off their skills, and the stands that can hold roughly 85,000 spectators. Once the party has started, however, everything is dwarfed by the joy of having fun, the music, the colors, and the desire to move to the rhythm of samba.

A PARTY OF MUSIC AND COLORS

A GREEN OASIS IN THE CITY

If you want to escape the confusion that dominates Rio de Janeiro and you don't feel like just relaxing on a beach, you can go explore an actual forest in Tijuca. This forest has a surface area of roughly 4,000 hectares fully covered in *mata atlântica*, the original forest of the coastal areas of south-eastern Brazil. This vegetation is more and more rare these days due to deforestation. Here you will find immense paths through greenery, waterfalls, and you might come across various animals, including colorful birds, iguanas, monkeys, and sloths.

SOCCER AS A WAY OF LIFE

Soccer and Brazil are one and the same. Brazil has one of the most formidable national teams in the world and some of the best players come from this nation. One towers above all the rest: the soccer legend Pelé, also known as *O Rei* (the King), who FIFA named Footballer of the Century. The reason for this success is easy to see. Everyone in this country plays soccer and not only on actual soccer pitches, but also on the streets and the beaches. Do you want some proof? Go to Copacabana and try not to get wrangled into playing soccer!

DID YOU KNOW THAT CHRIST THE REDEEMER...

Is a statue 124 feet high that weighs over 1000 tons.

Is located at the top of Corcovado, 2,300 feet above sea level.

Shows Christ in the pose of embracing all of humanity.

Can be reached by climbing up 222 steps or via 3 panoramic elevators and 8 escalators.

Features a plaque commemorating Marconi, the Italian scientist who sent the command to turn on its lights in 1931 via radio waves from Rome.

BUENOS AiRES

Right from the start, we were struck by the cheerful and friendly way we were greeted by the locals when walking through the streets of Buenos Aires. Aboard a horse-drawn carriage, with the driver telling us about the city's sights, we visited some historical locations, such as Plaza de Mayo and Avenida Cinco de Mayo, and the most important locations, like the obelisk and the Metropolitan Cathedral. After taking some photos in front of the Casa Rosada, we explored some of the city's more interesting neighborhoods, like the colorful Boca or the San Telmo district, where we saw some improvised tango shows. They were so amazing! In the time we had left, we went to the National Historical Museum and Puerto Madero. Finally, we just had to end the day with a dinner of *asado*, grilled meat: it was really good.

Argentina   Spanish   Megalopolis

1. Go for a ride in a *mateo* (horse-driven carriage) around the Palermo neighborhood.
2. Show off your kite-flying skills at Parque de los Niños.
3. Get your photo taken in front of the famous Casa Rosada, the seat of the government.
4. Explore the fabulous rooms of the Teatro Colón.
5. Stroll through the lively streets of La Boca, the colorful neighborhood.
6. Watch a tango show in the San Telmo neighborhood.
7. Watch the Puente de la Mujer opening to let ships pass through.
8. Imagine being an astronaut at the Galileo Galilei Planetarium.

95

GIULIA LOMBARDO

Is an illustrator who lives and works in Florence. After a classical high school diploma, she decided to completely change her course of studies following her passion and enrolling at Nemo Academy of Digital Arts in Florence, where she graduated with honors in 2013 as Entertainment Designer. Since then, she has worked as a freelance illustrator for children's books, as a graphic designer and a web designer. In the past years, she has illustrated several books for White Star Kids, with great enthusiasm and creativity.

FEDERICA MAGRIN

Born in Varese in 1978, has worked in publishing for over ten years, first as editor of Edizioni De Agostini and now as a freelance. She mainly works in children's books, but also writes educational texts and stories and translates novels.

Graphic layout
Maria Cucchi

WSKids
WHITE STAR KIDS

White Star Kids® is a registered trademark property of White Star s.r.l.

© 2018, 2019 White Star s.r.l.
Piazzale Luigi Cadorna, 6
20123 Milan, Italy
www.whitestar.it

Translation: Langue&Parole, Milan

Revised edition

ISBN 978-88-544-1463-1
1 2 3 4 5 6   23 22 21 20 19

Printed in China

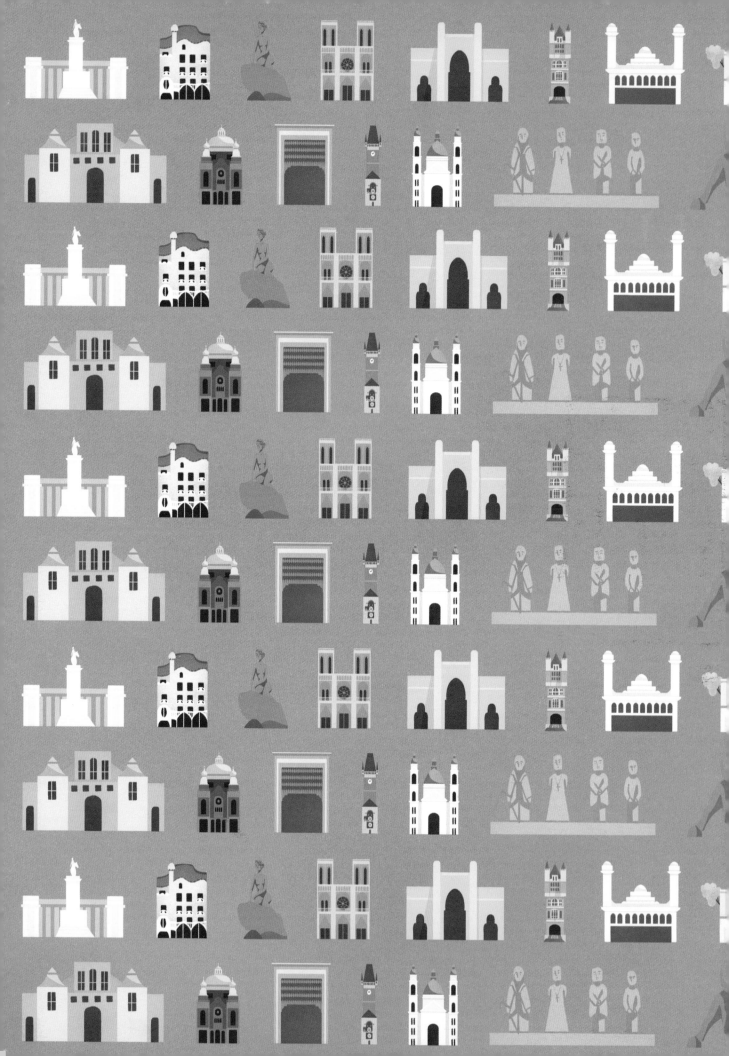